A New Year A New You

THE BOOK OF HEALTHY RESOLUTIONS

Acknowledgements

Cartoons by Tim Jaques
Recipes on pages 44, 46, 47, 49, 50 by kind permission of the Health Education Board for Scotland

© Health Education Authority, 1993
Hamilton House
Mabledon Place
WC1H 9TX

ISBN 1 85448 932 1

Typeset by Type Generation Ltd, London

Printed by Heronsgate Ltd, London and Essex

Contents

A new year, a new you	5
Getting active, feeling good	10
Eat well, feel well	27
Drinking sense	51
A smoke-free year?	61
Beating stress	72
Reducing your key health risks	83
Progress chart	92

A new year, a new you

Have you resolved to do something about your fitness, weight, smoking or anything else which affects your health?

This book is designed to help you take stock of your life and make up your mind how you'd like to change things. The first page asks you a few questions about the way you are now and there are quizzes and diaries in each section to help you assess your present lifestyle.

If you decide to do something positive, you will find hundreds of practical tips about ways of improving your health – about becoming the new you.

It's a challenge. Are you up to it? No don't just shut the book. This isn't intended for fitness fanatics who want to run a mile every day. It's a book for anyone who'd just like to feel better in themselves.

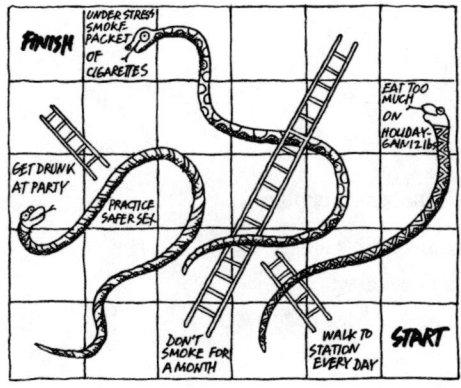

A new year, a new you

A healthy lifestyle?

Answer this quiz to see how healthy your present lifestyle is.

Circle one	How I would describe myself	See page
	My weight is:	29
a	Right for my height	
b	Under my correct weight	
c	Over my correct weight	
	My physical activity level:	11
a	Very active (exercise three times a week)	
b	Reasonably active (do something active when I can)	
c	Very inactive (hardly ever do anything active)	
	My smoking:	61
a	I don't smoke	
b	I want to give up	
c	I don't want to give up	
	My alcohol consumption:	55
a	I stick to sensible limits	
b	I need to cut down	
c	I get drunk at least once a week	

A new year, a new you

My stress level: 73

a Never stressed
b Sometimes stressed
c Stressed all the time

I eat: 33

a Regular balanced meals
b Too many fatty and sugary foods
c Anything which is to hand

I use safer sex: 87

a Always
b Sometimes
c Never

If you circle all '**c**'s you definitely need this book. Mostly '**b**'s, means there is room for improvement. All '**a**'s congratulations you are taking positive action to maintain good health.

A new year, a new you

Your health in your hands

There are all sorts of things you can do which will help to improve your own health. Obviously, it depends on where you're starting from, and on your individual circumstances. Although you can't avoid all causes of ill health and accidents, in broad terms, the best advice to everyone would be:

- If you smoke, do your very best to give up. It's the single most important thing you could do as far as your health is concerned.

  (Turn to pages 66–71 for tips on how to do it).

- If you're already a non-smoker, stay that way. You've got a head start.

- Be as physically active as you can. It helps your heart and you'll feel better for it. It will also help you control your weight – which in turn will put less strain on your heart. Maintaining your suppleness and strength are also essential elements of fitness.

  (See pages 10–26 for some interesting ideas on how to get more active).

- Enjoy your food but try to eat a balanced diet that will be good for you as well. You wouldn't put the wrong type of fuel in a car, would you? So be kind to your body and it will be kind to you.

  (You'll find plenty of ideas and menus to choose from by turning to pages 33–50)

- If you drink alcohol – as most people do – stick to recommended "sensible drinking" limits for average weekly consumption and you'll be able to enjoy your favourite drink without it doing you any harm. But remember, don't drink and drive.

  (See page 55 for details on safe drinking).

A new year, a new you

- Try to avoid getting too stressed – easier said than done perhaps, but there are techniques we can all use to recognise when stress is getting on top of us. If you do something about it early enough, the stress doesn't take over.

    (Ideas for you to try out can be found on pages 77–82)

- As far as your sex life is concerned, take sensible precautions and you'll minimise your risk of getting any of the infections that are passed on by sex, including HIV. Using a condom (male or female) is the best protection. Better safe than sorry.

- There are also things you can do to reduce your risk of cancer. We've already mentioned giving up smoking – that's a must. It's also a good idea not to expose yourself to too much sun – a cause of skin cancer – and to keep a look out for some of the early warning signs of cancer. A high fibre diet will reduce your risk of bowel cancer.

    (Turn to pages 84–86 for advice)

So there you have it – some of the very basic do's and don'ts about looking after yourself. Clearly, some illnesses and health problems can't be foreseen or even prevented. That's life. But we do have the ability to influence our own health in many, many ways. If you're interested in making the most of that ability, read on.

Getting active, feeling good

Being physically active is perfectly natural. Our bodies are made for it. We feel better both physically and mentally when we shake off that lethargic feeling and get moving. And if we do the right amount often enough, it helps to prevent heart disease and maintains our strength and flexibility.

It's decided then — you really want to shake off that lethargic feeling

Getting active, feeling good

How active are you?

Answer this quiz to find out how active you are.

	Tick which applies to you		
	Never	Sometimes	Always
Do you walk or cycle rather than take a bus or car when you can?	○	○	○
When you walk is it brisk?	○	○	○
Can you walk up a hill without getting too puffed?	○	○	○
Do you use the stairs instead of the lift?	○	○	○
Do you swim, dance, cycle or run regularly?	○	○	○
Can you reach a high shelf easily?	○	○	○
Can you carry shopping or a case easily without feeling breathless?	○	○	○
Each day are you active enough to get warm and breathe faster for several minutes?	○	○	○
Each week do you do something fairly energetic 2 or 3 times for about 20 to 30 minutes?	○	○	○

This is not all, the benefits for you could be:
- improving your health;
- feeling generally better in yourself – more relaxed and at ease;
- feeling energetic – better able to cope with life's daily challenges;
- controlling your weight and looking good for it;
- helping your heart, muscles and joints to do their job more efficiently;
- enjoying yourself with your friends, and making friends and contacts because you're out and about more.

You can see there's plenty to be gained by being physically active. Despite that, a recent nationwide survey found that seven out of ten men and eight out of ten women aren't physically active enough for their own health, even though most of them think they are.

So for most people there's scope for becoming more active than in the past. But don't worry, if you feel jogging is not for you, there are plenty of other ways of getting active.

So where do you start? The first thing is to work out how active – or otherwise – you really are and then try to do a little more each day. Choose an activity that's enjoyable and right for you.

How often and how much

If you haven't been active the first thing to do is to start to build more activity into your daily life. Throughout the day try to take the more active option whenever possible. Have you thought about walking up the stairs instead of taking the lift or walking to the shops instead of taking the car or bus? It really depends on your personal routine and what is realistic for you. When you have managed to be a bit more active in your daily life you might like to think about doing some more regular exercise such as swimming, cycling or aerobics. To get real benefit from physical activity, you need to do it often enough and for long enough. It means making your heart beat faster and making you feel hot and out of breath. You might also want to improve your flexibility and strength, important aspects of overall fitness.

Getting active, feeling good

Try this frequency test

How often are you getting really active these days? (Doing something which makes your heart beat faster and leaves you feeling warm and out of breath). Try this test.

✓ if this is you	Frequency	Comments
	More than three or four times a week?	You should be feeling better for it
	Three or four times a week on average?	Keep it up.
	Once or twice a week?	At least you're doing something but not really quite enough.
	Less than once a week?	Better start thinking how you're going to step things up
	Almost never?	Make a commitment. Get active now.

What is your target for doing more?

A new year, a new you

Getting started

You're convinced you need to do more but there's no point rushing headlong into something if you've been a bit on the inactive side up to now. It's a question of building up gradually.

Some useful tips:

- Always warm up before physical activity with a few gentle bends and stretches.
- Don't do anything for at least half an hour after a meal.
- If you've got a cold, temperature or sore throat, leave it until you feel better.
- Better safe than sorry. Stop if you feel pain, dizzy, sick or unusually tired. And if the symptoms persist or come back later, see your doctor.

Be sensible about your clothing

Make sure you wear comfortable clothes and a good, strong pair of shoes. In most cases, you probably won't need to buy anything new. But if you decide to do something that involves a lot of running or jumping, make sure you've got shoes, plimsolls or trainers which:

- have a thick, cushioned sole, especially at the heel;
- are wide enough for comfort and have plenty of room for your toes;
- have good arch support and a strong heel cup.

The golden rules of being active

1. Do what comes naturally – find a more active way of doing the things you usually do.
2. Build up gradually – take your time, be patient about your progress and don't over-do it in the early stages.
3. Be more active more often – try to be more active in your daily life, adding up to around thirty minutes each day.

Getting active, feeling good

Or, if you choose a more vigorous activity, try to do it at least three times a week for twenty minutes at a time.
4 Get into a bit of a sweat – When you start to sweat, then you've been really getting active.

Try to choose activities which:

- You enjoy.
- Make you feel good.
- You can do regularly without too much difficulty.
- You can fit easily into your everyday routine.
- Are convenient.
- You can do in all weathers and times of the year.

Try to choose activities you can do in all weathers and times of year

A new year, a new you

Activities to choose from

Just a few of the hundreds of activities you can choose are given in the table below. Depending on the activity you choose the type of benefit you get will vary. All exercise develops strength, suppleness and stamina but in varying amounts and it is important to cover all three.

Activities	**Stamina**	**Suppleness**	**Strength**
Badminton	**	***	**
Climbing stairs	***	*	**
Cricket	*	**	*
Cycling (hard)	****	**	***
Dancing (ballroom)	*	***	*
Dancing (disco)	***	****	*
Gardening (digging)	***	**	****
Football (soccer)	***	***	***
Golf	*	**	*
Hill walking	***	*	**
Housework	*	**	*
Jogging	****	**	**
Mowing the lawn	**	*	***
Squash	***	***	**
Swimming (hard)	****	****	****
Tennis	**	***	**
Walking (briskly)	***	*	**
Weight-lifting	*	*	****
Yoga	*	****	*

* No real effect	*** Very good effect
** Beneficial effect	**** Excellent effect

Getting active, feeling good

Strength is improved by activities which use the muscles repeatedly with some resistance such as swimming, climbing the stairs or push up exercises.

Suppleness is improved by activities which involve moving the joints and stretching the muscles. These should also be done before and after vigorous exercise.

Stamina (heart and lung fitness) is developed by vigorous exercise which gets you warm and a little out of breath such as running, cycling and aerobics.

Do you find it difficult to do up your shoe laces?

The table opposite gives you an idea of the benefits which result from different activities. Which one you go for is entirely up to you. But whichever one you choose, remember the effort which you put into it is important. You need to know and feel you've done some exercise – not to the extent that it hurts, though, as that would be defeating the object.

Your day-by-day getting active planner

This planner is intended to help start you on your way. When you've decided you're going to get active, write down exactly how to do it during the first seven days. There's also a column to record how you feel after your physical activity. Good luck!

	Type of activity	**Time taken**	**How I felt**
Day 1			
Day 2			
Day 3			
Day 4			
Day 5			
Day 6			
Day 7			

Congratulations! You've been at it for seven days now. The more you do, the easier it gets. Stick at it!

Getting active, feeling good

Exercises

Here are a few exercises which you could do on your own.

Exercising for suppleness

These are some simple stretching exercises. Do them at least three times a week and you'll begin to feel your body becoming more supple and relaxed. You should also do them to warm up before starting on anything more vigorous.

Points to bear in mind

- Do all stretching exercises slowly and smoothly.
- Repeat each one eight to twelve times.
- Doing them more times or more quickly won't have any extra benefit.
- You don't need to do twelve on the first day. Just do as many as you are comfortable with and gradually build up.
- If you have trouble with back pain, it might be advisable to see your doctor first. In any case, do these exercises very gently.
- You can do many of these exercises sitting or lying down, if you find them difficult standing up.

1 Shoulder circling

This is to maintain suppleness in your shoulders.

- Stand tall and relaxed with your arms at your sides.
- Slowly circle your right shoulder backwards.
- Repeat with your left shoulder.
- Continue on alternate sides.

2 Calf stretching

This is to stretch your calves and keep your ankles supple.

- Stand facing a wall, at arm's length from it.
- Place your hands on the wall for support.
- Stretch your right leg out straight behind you with the ball of your foot on the floor and your toes pointing towards the wall.
- Gently push your right heel towards the floor, allowing your left leg to bend as necessary (but no further than is shown in the picture).

3 Ankle reaching

This is to stretch your lower back and the backs of your thighs

- Sit on the floor with your legs straight in front of you and your knees as near to the floor as is comfortable.
- Place your hands on top of your thighs.
- Slowly and smoothly slide your hands down your legs as far as you can comfortably reach.
- Return to the upright position and repeat.
- Do not bounce into the movement.

Exercising for strength

These exercises are designed to help tone up your muscles to meet the more strenuous demands of daily life. You need strong arms for pushing, pulling and lifting. Strong stomach muscles are important for good posture and avoiding back pain. And you need strong legs for many things, including getting out of armchairs and baths, climbing stairs and running.

As you get older, it's especially important to maintain your strength in order to keep active and independent.

Points to bear in mind:

- Try to do these exercises every day, or at least twice a week.
- Don't push yourself too hard to start with.
- To start with repeat exercise 5–6 times.
- Build up gently and gradually to about 8–12 repeats.

1 Arms

These exercises strengthen mostly upper arms, shoulders and chest. There are three types; start with the first which is the easiest. If you can manage this exercise easily, do the following one the next time.

- Stand at arm's length from a wall.
- Place your hands shoulder width apart on the wall.
- Now bend your arms until your forehead touches the wall.
- Then push yourself away again until your arms are straight.

- Kneel on all fours.
- Move your hands forward slightly and take most of your weight on to them.
- Bend your arms and lower the top half of your body towards the floor.
- Only go as far as is comfortable, and be careful not to sag in the middle.
- Straighten your arms again and return to the starting position.

- If you can do the kneeling press ups easily, you may be ready to attempt a full press up.
- Follow the instructions for kneeling press ups but alter the starting position by lifting your knees off the floor, so that your weight is supported on your hands and toes and your body is in a straight line.

2 Stomach, back and hips

Weak muscles in the stomach and back put extra strain on your spine. These exercises will help to strengthen your stomach muscles, flatten any bulges and improve your posture.

Curl ups

These strengthen your stomach muscles.

- Lie on your back with your knees bent, and feet flat on the floor.
- Put your hands on top of your thighs.
- Lifting your head and shoulders off the floor, slide your fingers along your thighs a little.
- Then uncurl slowly back to the lying position.

As an alternative you can do this exercise lying on your back with your feet and lower legs on the seat of a chair.

Chest raises

These strengthen the muscles in your back.

- Lie on your stomach on the floor, with your head on one side.
- Slowly lift your head, neck and shoulders away from the floor.
- Only go as far as is comfortable.
- Slowly relax down.
- Repeat the whole exercise.

A new year, a new you

Leg lifts

These strengthen your hips and back

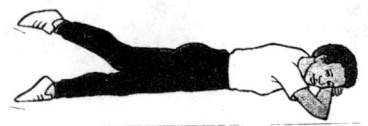

- Lie on your stomach on the floor.
- Slowly lift your right leg away from the floor, as far as is comfortable.
- Slowly relax down, and repeat with the other leg.

As an alternative, start on all fours and slowly stretch one leg back. Repeat with the other leg.

3 Legs

These leg exercises will help you tone up and strengthen your thighs, calves and bottom. They are particularly important for older people.

- Sit on a firm kitchen chair.
- Stand up, without using your hands and without leaning forward too much.
- Make sure your legs straighten completely.
- Sit down again and repeat.
- Gradually progress to just touching the chair instead of sitting down each time.

Alternatively try this exercise.

- Stand at the bottom of a flight of stairs.
- Step up on to the first step, making sure you straighten both legs.
- Step down again.
- Do this with alternate legs.

Getting active, feeling good

Exercising for stamina

You can build up your stamina (heart and lung fitness) at home in a variety of ways.

- Running on the spot.
- Walking or running up and down stairs.
- Skipping with a rope.

You could try using a home exercise machine. But these can be very expensive and are not really necessary. In any event, try one out at a sports centre and ask for advice before buying anything.

A simple stamina test

If, for at least two months, you've been exercising to improve your stamina and you want to measure your progress, you could try this test.

1 Find a safe, reasonably flat route about one mile long.
2 Put on comfortable clothes and a pair of running shoes and take a watch.
3 Walking, or running, or using a mixture of both, cover the mile as quickly as you can without getting uncomfortably breathless.
4 Aim for a pace you can keep up. It's likely to take most people between 10 and 20 minutes.
5 If you have any pain or discomfort, stop immediately.
6 If you are over 55 or have not been very physically active until recently – and if it's the first time you've taken the test – it's best to walk all the way.
7 Note down or remember the time it takes you to cover the mile.
8 Repeat the test every month or so to see how you are getting on. You'll be able to compare your performances.
9 Remember, to stay fit, you need to keep it up.
10 It's not so much the number of minutes you take that matters but the fact that, over time, you're able to do better. The fact that you feel better in yourself is probably the most important thing.

A new year, a new you

The 'talk-test'
You should be able to talk or whistle throughout any exercise/activity. You should be able to hold a conversation while walking, jogging, cycling, or performing any other aerobic activity. If talking or whistling is difficult or impossible, it indicates that the exercise is too intense for your current state of health and fitness.

How have you been getting on?

When you've been more physically active for a few weeks, it could be interesting to check out your own progress. Fill in the checklist below:

	No. of days I've been active	No. of minutes per week	Type of activity
week 1			
week 2			
week 3			
week 4			

Don't give up. Remember that you may have been inactive for quite some time. But it's never too late to put things right. Think about what you can gain and go for it. Being in good condition is something that we can all aim for and achieve.

Eat well, feel well

You are what you eat. Where have you heard that before? The plain fact is that many of us don't eat the right balance of food. That's really what it's all about – not doing anything to excess and making sure we try and eat a bit more of some things and a bit less of others. If you eat well, you'll probably feel well. The question is: what should we eat? And are there "naughty but nice" items that ought to be consigned straight away to bin? And remember, healthy eating doesn't have to be expensive or difficult to prepare.

Enjoy your food – some golden rules

Food is there to be enjoyed. But there are some golden rules of eating which will enable you to enjoy what you eat at the same time as eating healthily:

- Eat a variety of foods. Don't get into the rut of eating the same thing day in day out.
- Eat the right amount to be a healthy weight. (See page 29)
- Eat plenty of foods that are rich in starch and fibre. (See page 38)
- Don't eat too much fat – and if you're doing the cooking, try to cut down on the amount you use. (See page 37)
- Don't eat sugary foods too often.
- Eat plenty of fruit and vegetables.
- Make sure you get enough vitamins and minerals in your food.
- If you drink alcohol, keep within sensible limits. (See page 55)
- Cut down on the amount of salt you use in cooking and don't add extra at the table.

A new year, a new you

What weight should I be?

It's fair to say that many people spend a lot of time these days worrying about their weight – or is it shape? But from the health point of view, there's a happy balance to be struck. It's not a question of us all looking like beanpoles, fashion models or film stars. It's a question of not getting overweight and putting too much strain on our hearts and bodies. If you are overweight your risk of heart and lung problems, diabetes and arthritis are increased.

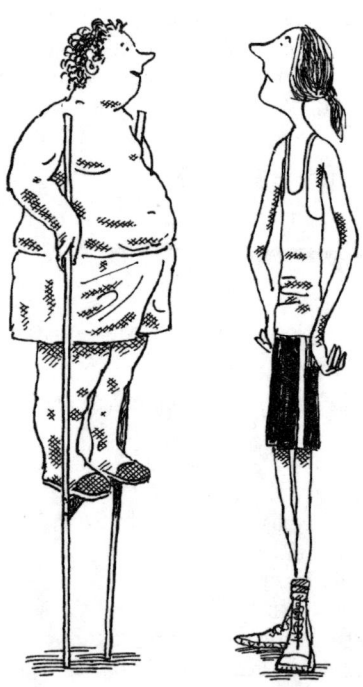

Are you the right height for your weight?

Eat well, feel well

Are you the right weight for your height?

How to find out

The chart on this page will give you an indication of how much you should weigh in relation to your height. Find out where you are in the chart and you'll see whether you are within the broadly acceptable range or whether you need to lose some weight. The pinch test is also a good guide as to whether you need to lose weight.

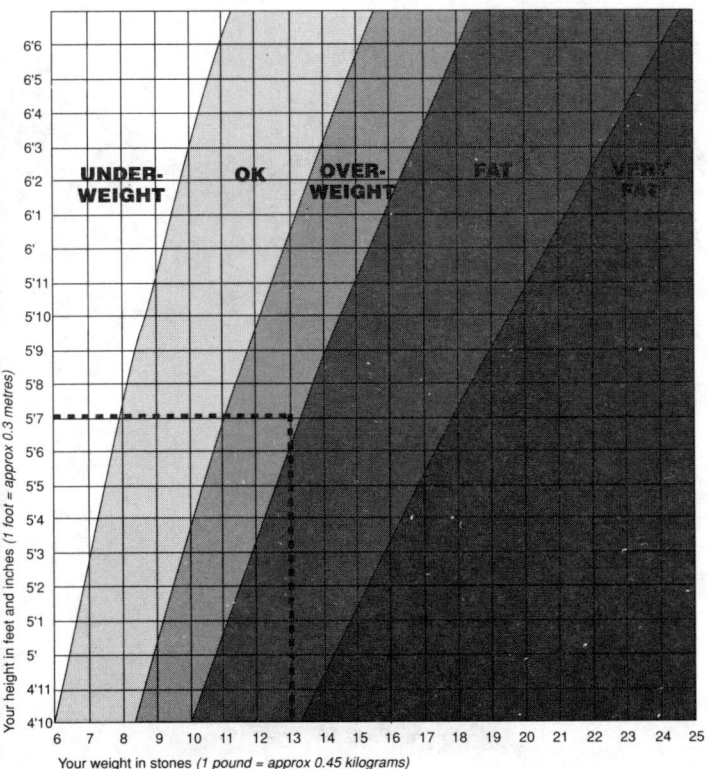

A new year, a new you

Pinch test

Nearly half our body fat is found just under the surface of the skin. Measuring the amount of fat in certain places is a good way to determine your overall body fat. This can be done by getting someone to place their thumb and forefinger approximately 3 centimetres apart on the back of your right arm, and pinching gently. Ask them then to measure the pinched skin. Readings of over 2.5 cm for a woman and 2 cm for a man shows the amount of fat is high. The same test can be used on the back, the abdomen or the inner thigh.

Changing for good

Don't panic, though. Losing weight should be done gradually and carefully. Crash diets often mean that you put the weight back on later. What you want is slowly but surely to change the balance of your food – not just for a few weeks but for good.

Look at your diary

Are there times when you are tempted to snack.

Do you always eat in front of the TV and not notice what you eat?

Do you always eat in front of the TV and not notice what you eat?

Can you identify foods which contain a lot of fat or sugar you eat frequently?

Look at the labels on packets and tins to see how much fat and sugar they contain. Sugar is listed under carbohydrates.

Before you can do anything about eating for health, you need to know what you eat right now.

A new year, a new you

What do you eat?

Keep a record over a week of the things you eat both at mealtimes and between meals.

Date	Time	How much	What	Where	Mood

Eat well, feel well

Making Healthy Choices

A balanced diet

A healthy eating pattern will include the correct balance of foods from the four main food groups. If you choose foods in these proportions you will get all your nutritional needs.

The amount of food you need daily depends on your age, sex, how active you are and if you are overweight. You need to reduce your daily intake in order to lose weight.

Four food groups	Servings per day	Serving size
Bread, cereal, potato	5–11	3 tbs of breakfast cereal slice of bread 1 tbs of rice/pasta/noodles 1 medium sized potato
Vegetables and fruit	5–9	½ cup cooked, 1 cup raw, 1 piece fruit or small salad
Milk, cheese, yoghurt	2–3	small pot yoghurt/cottage cheese/fromage frais, ⅓ pt semi skimmed milk, 1½ oz/40g cheese
Meat and alternatives e.g. fish, nuts	2–3	2–3oz/50–70g meat or oily fish, 2 eggs, 4-5 oz white fish, 3 tbs cooked beans, pulses, lentils, 2 tbs nuts
Fats	0–3	1 tsp butter/marg, 1 tsp oily salad dressing/mayonnaise, 1 tsp cooking oil

A new year, a new you

Fat in food

This table shows the amount of fat there is in one serving of some foods, along with the fat content of some lower fat alternatives choices.

Meat and meat products

Pork chop (85 g or 3 oz serving)

fried with fat left on	16 g
grilled with fat removed	6 g

Sausage (2 large)

ordinary	21 g
low fat'	11 g

Beefburgers, grilled (2)

ordinary	18 g
'low fat'	9 g

Fish

Cod (85 g or 3 oz serving)

fried in batter	9 g
poached	1 g

Fish fingers (3)

fried	11 g
grilled	6 g

Poultry

Roast chicken (85 g or 3 oz)

skin left on	12 g
skin removed	5 g

Fats and oils

Spreads (10 g or ½ oz serving)

butter	8 g
margarine (all types)	8 g
low fat spread	4 g
ghee	10 g
oil (all types)	10 g

Dairy products

Milk (284 ml or ½ pt)

whole	11 g
semi skimmed	5 g
skimmed	0.3 g

Cheese (60 g or 2 oz serving)

Cheddar	20 g
Edam	14 g
low fat Cheddar	8 g

Cream (30 g or 1 oz serving)

double cream	14 g
single cream	6 g
yoghurt (low-fat plain)	0.3 g
fromage frais (low fat)	0.3 g

Starchy foods

Potatoes (140 g or 5 oz serving)

thin-cut chips	17 g
thick-cut chips	8 g
oven chips	7 g
roast potatoes	8 g
baked potatoes	0.1 g
boiled potatoes	0.1 g

Rice (85 g or 3 oz raw weight)

fried	8 g
boiled	1 g

Chapattis

made with fat	8 g
made without fat	0.5 g

Sweet snacks

small chocolate bar	15 g
halva	11 g
sevyiaan	7 g
burfi	5 g
2 digestive biscuits	6 g

Savoury snacks

1 samosa	26 g
crisps (small bag)	
ordinary	9 g
'low fat'	7 g
Peanuts (small bag)	12 g
Chinese pastry with bean filling	6 g

A new year, a new you

Changes you may need to make

- Increase the number of daily measures from the vegetable and fruit and bread, cereal and potato groups. The foods rich in fibre.
- Reduce fatty and sugary foods.

Ways to eat less fat

By making simple changes to the type of food you eat and the ways that you prepare and cook it, will help you to eat less fat.

Try most of these tips and see how easy it can be to eat less fat:

- Choose a low fat spread rather than butter, hard margarine or ordinary soft margarine. Or use a margarine labelled 'high in polyunsaturates' – but remember, this type of margarine contains the same amount of fat and calories as butter, it is the type of fat which is different. If you do use butter or ordinary margarine, make sure you spread it more thinly.
- Buy skimmed or semi-skimmed milk rather than whole milk (silver top). Both have just as much calcium and protein as ordinary milk but much less fat.
- Use low fat yoghurt or fromage frais instead of cream, evaporated or condensed milk. If you do use cream, choose single rather than double. Remember, some artificial creams have as much fat as real cream.
- Try half-fat hard cheese or cottage cheese instead of ordinary cheese.
- Make salad dressings with yoghurt, herbs, spices, vinegar and lemon juice rather than mayonnaise or salad cream or choose the low fat types.
- Cut down on crisps, chocolate, cakes and biscuits. Try some of the suggestions for healthier snacks on page 40.
- Eat fish more often. Steam, grill, microwave or bake rather than deep frying in batter.
- Chicken and turkey are low in fat if the skin is removed, as most fat is just under the skin.
- Buy the leanest cuts of meat you can afford and trim off any remaining fat. Or use smaller quantities of lean meat and fill up on vegetables, potatoes or pulses (beans, peas, etc.)

Eat well, feel well

Cooking methods

The way food is cooked can affect the amount of fat and the amount of nutrients which are left after cooking. One excellent way of cooking is to use a steamer. This enables you to cook two things at once. For example rice in the bottom and vegetables above or vegetables and some fish with a dash of lemon juice and seasoning on top.

Other ways in which you might try to reduce fat are:

- Microwave, steam or grill instead of roasting and frying. If you do fry, use a non-stick pan and you may not need to use any fat or oil.
- Use a steep-sided, round bottomed pan like a wok to stir fry and you'll only need to use a small amount of oil.
- Casseroling or stewing are good ways to cook cheaper cuts of meat. Remove visible fat and spoon off any fat that comes to the surface. Remember to skin chicken and turkey before cooking.
- Mince can be very fatty even if it doesn't seem to be. Remove a lot of the fat by dry frying the mince (that is, without using any fat or oil) and then pouring off the excess fat. Or add cold water to the mince, bring it to the boil and then pour off the water. Either way, you can then use the mince in the normal way.
- Use less ghee butter in curries and drain off all visible fat.
- Take the fat off the surface of gravy. Let it stand for a few minutes, then spoon the fat off. Or use a gravy pourer which leaves the fat behind.
- Use as little oil and fat as possible for cooking. Choose one that is low in saturates and high in unsaturates, e.g. sunflower, soya, corn, rapeseed or olive oil.
- If you cook chips, cut them thick and straight and fry them in an oil that is high in unsaturates. Change the oil often. Or use oven chips instead which are lower in fat (see page 34).

A new year, a new you

How to eat plenty of starch and fibre

If you cut down on fat, you also cut down on calories. This is good if you want to lose weight. If you don't want to lose weight, then it is important to replace the calories with starchy foods which are high in fibre. Even if you do want to lose weight, you should still include some of these foods in your diet as they are filling without providing too many calories. Starch and sugar are both carbohydrates, but starch is used up slowly so that it stops you feeling hungry for a long time. Sugars give you an energy boost but you feel hungry again very soon.

Breakfast cereals are a good source of starch and fibre

Eat well, feel well

To increase the starch and fibre in your diet:

- Eat plenty of bread, chapattis or pitta bread – preferably wholemeal.
- Try crumpets, muffins, pikelets and scones, especially wholemeal varieties either at breakfast or as a snack. Use low fat spread or polyunsaturated margarine spread thinly.
- Eat more baked or boiled potatoes (but without added butter or cheese).
- Try sweet potatoes and plantains.
- Rice, particularly brown rice, is a good choice.
- Try dishes based on pasta, especially wholewheat pasta.
- Breakfast cereals are a good source of starch and fibre. Go for one with wholegrain ingredients and avoid the sugar-coated ones.
- Use wholemeal flour instead of white flour for baking. Or try half and half.
- Baked beans are a quick, easy and cheap way of getting fibre.
- Use more peas, beans and lentils. In many meals you can replace some of the meat with beans – it's much cheaper and very nutritious. There are many types of tinned beans and they are quick and easy to prepare.

Fruit and vegetables

Fruit and vegetables are good sources of fibre as well as many minerals and vitamins.

- Try to include more fruit and vegetables each day.
- Don't throw away all of the vitamins with the cooking water. Cook them in a steamer or cook them for a short time in as little water as possible, or use a steamer or microwave oven.
- Fresh fruit and vegetables are always in plentiful supply but those in season will probably be cheaper.
- For those not in season it's often cheaper to buy the frozen variety.
- Or try tinned vegetables with no added salt or sugar and fruit tinned in natural juices with no added sugar, rather than paying extra for imported fresh produce.

A new year, a new you

Snacks

Foods that are often eaten as snacks, like crisps, chocolate, cakes and biscuits are high in fat. Why not try some of these instead:

- Fresh fruit.
- Fresh or canned fruit in natural juice with plain low fat yoghurt.
- Scones, currant buns without icing or teabreads served plain or with a scraping of low fat spread or polyunsaturated margarine.
- Plain popcorn sprinkled with paprika and a little half-fat cheese.
- Roast sweetcorn or chickpeas
- Sticks of raw vegetables, like celery, carrot, peppers, cucumber and other salad vegetables.
- Low fat, low sugar yoghurts.
- Nuts without added salt.

If you're really hungry between meals try:

- Crispbread, rolls, pitta breads or sandwiches with mashed banana, half-fat cheese, cottage cheese, tuna, lean meat or chopped raw vegetables.
- Toast with a scraping of sugar free peanut butter.
- Pasta salad, e.g. pasta shells or twirls, red and green peppers, cucumber, sweetcorn, cold chopped chicken, or tuna or half-fat cheese.
- Bread rolls, french bread, pitta bread or scone base made into mini pizza using half-fat hard cheese, tomatoes, mushrooms and mixed herbs.
- Sugar-free breakfast cereals with semi-skimmed or skimmed milk.

Some ideas for your first week of really healthy eating

A common complaint by people who want to eat healthily is that no-one gives them specific ideas – the advice is all very general. So, here is a menu plan and a few recipes for you to try in your first week of *really* healthy eating. Remember, though, they're only suggestions.

Eat well, feel well

A week's healthy meals

MONDAY

Breakfast   Unsweetened muesli with skimmed/semi skimmed milk and sliced banana

Midday   Tuna and salad filled wholemeal rolls

Fruit scone

Evening   Vegetable lasagne with a green salad

2 scoops of low fat/low sugar frozen yoghurt

TUESDAY

Breakfast   Fresh grapefruit halves, lightly sprinkled with ground ginger and grilled

Midday   Jacket potato with baked beans (no butter)

Low fat/low sugar yoghurt

Evening   Chinese chicken served with noodles or boiled rice

Fresh fruit salad with low fat natural fromage frais

WEDNESDAY

Breakfast   Grilled tomatoes on thick slices of wholemeal toast

Midday   Pitta breads filled with shredded cabbage, carrot, lettuce and reduced fat cheddar type cheese

Currant bun

Evening   Mediterranean stew with boiled brown rice

Dried fruit compote

A new year, a new you

THURSDAY

Breakfast Unsweetened muesli with skimmed/semi skimmed milk

Fruit juice

Midday Sardines in tomato sauce on thick slices of wholemeal toast

Piece of fruit

Evening Stuffed green peppers served with potatoes or salad and wholemeal bread

Reduced fat/and sugar bread pudding

FRIDAY

Breakfast Low fat natural yoghurt with fresh fruit and a sprinkling of unsweetened muesli

Fresh fruit juice

Midday Chunky vegetable or lentil soup with wholemeal rolls

Piece of fruit

Evening Tuna, broccoli and pasta bake with salad or vegetables

Yoghurt jellies

SATURDAY

Breakfast Porridge made with skimmed/semi skimmed milk

Midday Slice of pizza (thick bread base and vegetable topping) with salad

Piece of fruit

Evening Spicy chicken casserole with boiled rice and vegetables

Baked banana with low fat natural yoghurt

SUNDAY	
Breakfast	2 lean, unsmoked bacon rashers grilled with grilled tomatoes and scrambled eggs and wholemeal rolls
Midday	French bread filled with cottage cheese and chives and salad
	Piece of fruit
Evening	Beef goulash and beans with jacket or new potatoes and vegetables
	Rice pudding made with skimmed/semi skimmed milk

'I thought it was supposed to be unsmoked bacon'

Vegetable lasagne

Ingredients: serves 4–6
8oz/225g wholewheat lasagne
8oz/225g onions, peeled
6oz/175g celery, cleaned
4oz/100g green pepper, de-seeded
8oz/225g carrots, washed
1lb/500g tin tomatoes
black pepper, salt to taste
oregano to taste

Sauce
2oz/50g polyunsaturated margarine
2oz/50g cornflour
1¼pt/750ml skimmed milk
10oz/275g low fat cottage cheese, sieved

Heat oven to 350°F/180°C, Gas No. 4.

Cook lasagne according to pack instructions; then drain and refresh in cold water.

Place onion, celery, pepper, carrots and tomatoes in a saucepan and bring to boil. Simmer for 10 minutes. Season with black pepper and oregano.

Make the sauce by melting the margarine, then add cornflour and stir till smooth. Add milk, stir until thickened and add cottage cheese. Simmer for 1 minute.

Layer lasagne and vegetable sauce in oven-proof dish, finishing with a layer of lasagne and cover with cheese sauce. Cook for 40 minutes or until browned.

Chinese chicken

Ingredients: serves 4
1lb/450g chicken breast meat with skin removed, finely sliced
2 tsp finely chopped fresh ginger (optional)
1–2 tblsp polyunsaturated oil (e.g. sunflower oil)
4oz/100g celery, sliced
3oz/75g yellow pepper, sliced
3oz/75g carrot, sliced
4oz/100g mushrooms, sliced
2oz/50g spring onion, sliced
1 x 8oz/227g can pineapple pieces in natural juice
3 floz/75ml chicken stock
2 tsp cornflour
4oz/100g bean sprouts
black pepper, to season

Using a large frying pan or wok, stir fry the chicken (with skin removed) with the ginger in 1 tblsp of hot polyunsaturated oil.

Cook for 2–3 minutes and then remove the cooked chicken with a slotted spoon. Keep it on a warm plate.

If all the oil is gone, add the other spoonful of polyunsaturated oil to the pan and stir fry the celery, yellow pepper, carrot, mushrooms and spring onions for 5–6 minutes. Put the chicken back in the pan.

Drain the pineapple and keep the juice. Mix together the cornflour and the chicken stock, and then add the pineapple juice. Pour the liquid into the pan and bring to the boil. Stir until the mixture has thickened.

Add the pineapple pieces and bean sprouts to the chicken mixture and heat through thoroughly. Season to taste. Serve with brown rice.

You can also use turkey breast in this delicious meal.

Mediterranean stew

Ingredients: serves 4-6

3 tbsp polyunsaturated margarine
4oz/100g onions, sliced
1½ lbs/675g lean shoulder steak cut into 1"/2.5cm cubes
16floz/480ml water
4 tbsp tomato puree
2 tbsp raisins
2 tbsp wine vinegar
2 tbsp red wine (optional)
1 tsp honey
1 garlic clove, crushed
2 bay leaves
1 cinnamon stick or pinch ground cinnamon
¼ tsp ground cloves and cumin

Melt margarine in a saucepan, add onions and steak and cook for 5 minutes, stirring all the time. Add remaining ingredients and stir to combine.

Cover and simmer over low heat for 2–2½ hours, stirring occasionally. Remove bay leaves and cinnamon stick before serving. Garnish with bay leaves if desired.

Serve with brown rice.

Stuffed green peppers

Ingredients: serves 4
6oz/175g brown rice
½pt/300ml boiling water
salt
4 tomatoes, skinned and chopped or canned tomatoes
1 onion grated
2oz/50g pine nuts (optional)
1oz/25g seedless raisins
4oz/100g low fat cheddar cheese grated
2 tbsp parsley, chopped
pinch of ground cinnamon
freshly ground black pepper
4 green peppers, cored and seeded, tops reserved
5 tbsp of water

If you are not using a steamer heat oven to 375°F /190°C, Gas No. 5

Cook the rice in boiling salted water for 30 minutes or until rice is tender and all water has been absorbed.

Remove from the heat and gently fold in tomatoes, onion, pine nuts and raisins. Fold in most of the cheese, reserving a little for the topping, then fold in parsley, cinnamon, salt and pepper to taste.

Stand the peppers upright in a steamer, cutting the bottoms if necessary. (Or put in a baking dish and cover with foil.)

Divide the filling equally between the peppers, sprinkle with the remaining cheese and replace the lids.

Pour water into the bottom of the steamer (or dish) and cook for 30–40 minutes, until the peppers are tender.

Serve with potatoes, which can be cooked in the bottom of the steamer or with a salad and wholemeal bread.

Tuna, broccoli and pasta bake

Ingredients: serves 4
8oz/225g pasta twists
6oz/175g broccoli pieces or 'florets'
1 x 14oz/400g can tuna fish in brine, drained

Cheese sauce
2oz/50g sunflower margarine
2oz/50g wholewheat flour or plain flour
1pt/600ml skimmed milk
3oz/75g low fat cheddar type cheese
½ tsp English mustard powder (optional)
black pepper, to season

Topping
1oz/25g fresh wholemeal breadcrumbs

Cook the pasta in boiling water for 5 minutes and then add the bite-size broccoli florets. Return to the boil and cook for another 4–5 minutes until the pasta and broccoli are just tender. Drain.

Flake the tuna fish over the bottom of an ovenproof dish.

To make the cheese sauce, put the margarine, flour and milk in a saucepan and heat gently until the margarine has melted. Turn the heat up and stir continuously until the sauce boils and thickens. Simmer for 2–3 minutes, then remove from the heat and stir in half of the cheese, the mustard and season with pepper.

Arrange the pasta and broccoli over the tuna and cover with the sauce. Mix together the breadcrumbs with the remaining cheese and sprinkle over the top.

Bake in an oven preheated to Gas No. 6/200°C/400°F for about 25 minutes, until the top is golden and crisp. Serve with lightly grilled tomatoes.

Spicy chicken casserole
Ingredients: serves 4
2 medium onions, finely chopped
8oz/225g small mushrooms (sliced)
2 tbsp polyunsaturated oil
2 tbsp wholewheat flour
½ tsp grated nutmeg
1 tsp ground ginger
½ pt/300ml chicken stock
½ pt/300ml skimmed or semi-skimmed milk
1-1½ lbs/600g cooked, skinless, chicken meat, chopped
1½–2oz/40–50g toasted almond flakes
freshly ground black pepper to taste

Fry onions and mushrooms in oil for 5–10 minutes or till soft. Add flour, nutmeg and ginger. Bring mixture to boiling point and cook for 1 minute. Blend in stock and milk, very slowly, and bring to the boil stirring constantly.

Add cooked chicken and pepper. Cover and simmer gently for approximately 30 minutes. Put mixture into a hot serving bowl and sprinkle on toasted almonds.

Serve with brown rice and salad. Garnish with spring onions.

A new year, a new you

Beef goulash with beans
Ingredients: serves 4–6
1lb/450g lean shoulder steak trimmed of fat and cubed
2 tbsp polyunsaturated oil
8oz/225g onion, sliced
2 sticks celery, sliced
2–3 tsp paprika
10floz/250 ml beef stock
8oz/225g can tomatoes, chopped
14oz/400g can red kidney beans, drained

Heat the oil in saucepan. Brown the meat. Add onions and celery. Stir in paprika. Add beef stock and tomatoes, season, cover and bake for 1 hour at 350°F/180°C, Gas No. 4. Add drained kidney beans and cook for 20 minutes.

Drinking sense

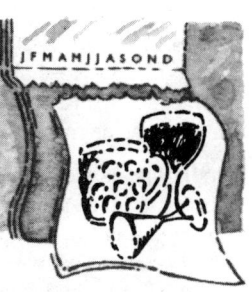

Been to lots of parties lately? But feeling you've had a bit too much booze for your own good? Now's the perfect moment, to step back and take a look at your own drinking. Nobody's saying "give it up". Most people can enjoy alcohol without problems. There are sensible limits, though, to how much you should be drinking and how often. If you'd like to see how you measure up, read on....

Do you know your drinks?

It may sound a funny question but it's important to know the amount of alcohol in your drinks and how the different drinks compare with each other. The drinks shown below, in normal pub measures, each contain roughly the same amount of alcohol. You can think of each one as a unit.

1 unit =

 ½ pint of ordinary beer, lager or cider

 a single measure of spirits (whisky, gin, bacardi, vodka, etc.)

 a small glass of wine

 a small glass of sherry

 a measure of vermouth or aperitif

A new year, a new you

Don't believe it? Well, it's true. So the beer and lager drinkers aren't drinking less alcohol. They're just taking it in another form. And by the way, extra strength lagers contain around three times as much alcohol (8–10%) as ordinary lager.

Alcohol is also loaded with calories that go straight into the bloodstream. A pint of ordinary beer contains 180 calories. Add those onto your food intake and you can see how easy it is to become overweight. The table below gives a rough idea of the calories in different drinks.

Beers, lager & cider (half pint)	**Calories**
bitter	90
light or mild ale	70
ordinary strength lager	85
dry cider	95
sweet cider	110
Spirits (1 pub measure)	
brandy, whisky, gin, rum or vodka	50
Wine (an average glass)	
dry, white or red	75
sweet white	100
Sherry (1 pub measure)	
dry	55
medium	60
cream	70

How much do you really drink?

That's the first question you need to ask. We're not talking about the Christmas and New Year period. That's probably not typical. But in an average week, what do you reckon? Is it ten pints? Twenty glasses of wine? Forty single measures of spirits? Eighty pints? More?

Drinking sense

Remember to include all your drinks and not just the ones you have in the evening

Do you really know how much you drink? Don't just guess. Fill in the drinking diary on the next page. Either fill it in for last week or start the diary today and write down all the drinks you have this week. Remember to include all your drinks, not just the ones you have in the evening. Don't cheat. And don't make excuses about it not being a typical week.

Count how many units of alcohol you had each day and add up your total score for the week. Then compare your score with the sensible limits on the following page.

Also, note down when and where you drank and who you were with. If you think you need to cut down, it will help you to work out how to go about it.

A message for home drinkers

Another word of caution. People who drink at home tend to give themselves more generous measures than they'd otherwise get in a pub. Take that into account when you're recording how much you drink.

When you've got a better idea of your drinking habits, what's your reaction? Do you feel it's OK? Or is there a niggling doubt in your mind? Perhaps you'd like to cut down a bit. Knowing when and with whom you drink most will help you plan ahead.

A new year, a new you

My drinking diary

Day	What	Where/When/Who with	Units	Total
Monday				
Tuesday				
Wednesday				
Thursday				
Friday				
Saturday				
Sunday				
Total for the Week				

So what's a sensible limit?

Assuming that you want to carry on enjoying a drink without it doing you any harm, you ought to try and stick within the following weekly limits

- 21 units of alcohol per week for men
- 14 units of alcohol per week for women

One of the reasons for this difference is that in women only 45 to 55 per cent of the body weight is made up of water whereas in men it is between 55 and 65 per cent. As alcohol is distributed through the body fluids it is more diluted in men.

Bear in mind that the above limits are weekly limits. It's usually better to spread your drinking out over four or five days. No sudden binges.

In any event, it does your body good to have a few alcohol-free days. Try to keep at least two days like that every week.

A new year, a new you

The risks for heavy drinkers

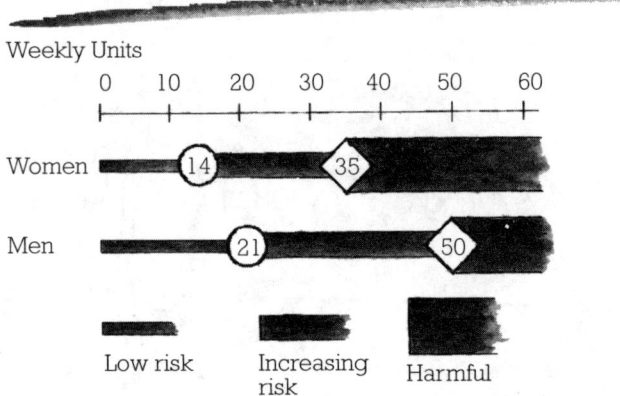

Studies have shown that, to a greater or lesser degree, alcohol consumption may be linked to the following:

Liver disease
Deaths from liver disease (cirrhosis) are ten times higher among heavy drinkers than non-drinkers.

Cancers
- mouth
- pharynx
- oesophagus
- liver
- larynx
- rectum
- colon

There's also an added risk if you smoke as well. The risk of developing cancer of the oesophagus may be 150 times greater in heavy drinkers and smokers than in those who abstain from both.

Heart disease and stroke
Heavy drinkers also increase their risk of heart disease and stroke. See the chart below. The risk of a stroke among men who drink over 37 units a week could be between two and four times higher than non-drinkers.

Alcohol dependence

If your consumption is very high, you could be heading towards alcoholism. No, not me, you may be muttering. But alcoholism can happen to anyone. In practice an alcoholic is someone who can't do without alcohol. Who's totally dependent on it. It would end up running your life and, if nothing is done abut it, could ruin your life and health.

What you will gain by drinking less

Cutting down now means:

1. Less risk of having an accident, developing high blood pressure or liver disease.
2. Less risk of being overweight.
3. Improved concentration and a clear head.
4. Fewer hangovers, headaches and stomach upsets.
5. Sounder sleep and less tiredness generally.
6. New sense of being in control and feeling fitter.
7. Time and energy for activities other than drinking.
8. Fewer arguments and rows with friends or family.
9. More pleasure out of your sex life.
10. If you're trying for a baby, cutting down on drink will improve your chances of success, whether you're a man or a woman.
11. If you're pregnant, your baby will stand a better chance of being born healthy. During pregnancy you should cut down as much as possible, 1 or 2 units a week – or stop drinking alcohol altogether until after the baby is born.
12. More money. Work out how much you've spent on alcohol during the last week.

When to give alcohol a miss altogether

There are certain times and situations when drinking alcohol is just not appropriate because it will put either yourself or other people at risk. So the motto is – Enjoy your drink by all means but don't drink when:

- **You are going to be driving a car.**
- **You are in charge of machinery.**
- **You need your powers of concentration – at work, for example.**

If you have just one drink, your chances of having an accident are increased. One in five drivers killed in road accidents are over the legal limit. So cut it out altogether at work and leave the car at home if you're going out for a drink, unless someone's willing to drive you who will stick to soft drinks for the evening.

Don't forget that it takes one hour for the body to get rid of one unit of alcohol. So you can still be unfit to drive the morning after a heavy drinking session.

Hangovers

Hangovers are caused by drinking too much alcohol. Dehydration is one of the problems. The alcohol which you drink tends to make the water move out of the body cells. Drinking plenty of water when you go to bed can help, but the only way of avoiding a hangover is to be careful how much you drink.

How much do you know about alcohol?

1. How long does it take for the body to absorb one unit of alcohol?
   - **a** 2 hours
   - **b** 1 hour
   - **c** 30 minutes
   - **d** 15 minutes

2. Which of these things affect the concentration of alcohol in your blood?
   - **a** Your height
   - **b** Your weight
   - **c** Your age
   - **d** Your sex
   - **e** All of these

3. Which is correct?
   - **a** Alcohol is a depressant
   - **b** Alcohol is a stimulant

4. If a man drank 4 pints of beer how long would it take for his blood alcohol to return to zero?
   - **a** 12 hours
   - **b** 8 hours
   - **c** 4 hours
   - **d** 2 hours

5. Which of these drinks contain the highest number of calories?
   - **a** Half a pint of bitter
   - **b** Half a pint of dry cider
   - **c** Measure of rum
   - **d** Dry white wine
   - **e** Glass of sweet sherry

6. Which of these brain functions are affected by alcohol?
   - **a** Judgment
   - **b** Self-control
   - **c** Co-ordination
   - **d** None of these
   - **e** All of these

7. Which of these illnesses can be caused by excessive drinking?
   - **a** Stomach disorders
   - **b** Depression
   - **c** High blood pressure
   - **d** Vitamin deficiency
   - **e** Sexual difficulties
   - **f** Brain damage
   - **g** Hepatitis
   - **h** Cirrhosis
   - **i** Cancer of the mouth/throat
   - **j** All of these
   - **k** None of these

Answers: 1d 2e 3a 4b 5b 6e 7j

A new year, a new you

Personal drinking rules

It's a good idea to set yourself some personal drinking rules that keep you within the sensible drinking limits.

Exactly what those rules are only you can decide. The important thing is that they work. Here are some to choose from:

1 Keep a drink diary. It will help you keep track of what you're drinking.

2 Watch it at home. Try to avoid heading straight for a drink when you return from work. Find other ways to relax. (see page 78)

3 Don't be pressurised. Say no to other people if you don't really want another drink. And don't feel awkward about having a soft drink instead.

4 Avoid getting involved in buying rounds. It often means you end up drinking more.

5 Occupy yourself while drinking. It helps you to drink more slowly and cuts down the amount you consume.

6 Avoid drinking as a habit. Don't drink just because you're bored. Find other things to do.

7 Have days off. Keep at least two days a week as alcohol-free days.

8 Pace your drinks. Try spacing them out by having soft drinks occasionally.

9 Chart your progress over the weeks and see if you can gradually cut down.

10 Don't go over the limit you've set for yourself. Regard it as a matter of personal pride.

A smoke-free year?

So you really do want to give up smoking. That's not surprising. Most smokers do. And many, like you, feel the New Year's a good time to try. It may not exactly be easy, but millions of smokers have done it already, so there's no reason why you can't do it too. The key to success is really wanting to. If you've got the willpower, you'll do it. A few techniques will come in handy – this chapter will help you.

The four stages of stopping

If you're reading this, you must be interested in trying to stop. So how do you go about it? There's no miracle cure. But there are some tricks of the trade worth trying.

Basically, there are four stages you need to go through:

1 Think about why you want to stop – that's an essential first step and the key to your ultimate success.
2 Prepare yourself. It's got to be the right time and the right place.
3 Do it. Choose any day, and just stop. If you've prepared well, you can stick at it.
4 Stay stopped. Work at it. Don't give in. And before you know it, you'll be one of the vast majority of the population who are non-smokers.

So let's look in a bit more detail at each of the four stages.

A new year, a new you

Why do you want to stop?

The big question is – why do you really want to quit? Different people do it for different reasons. But it's useful for you to be clear about your reasons. They'll keep you going if you find things a bit hard during the first few days of stopping.

Tick the reasons in this checklist. Maybe put them in order of priority.

Reasons for stopping	**Priority ranking (1, 2, 3 etc)**
My health will be better.	
I'll smell fresher.	
I'll save a lot of money to spend on other things.	
I'll lose that awful smoker's cough.	
It'll be better for my children, who won't have to endure my cigarette smoke.	
I'll be nicer to be with as far as other people are concerned.	
I'll be able to run for the bus without getting out of breath.	

A smoke-free year?

Do you know the risks?

Smoking kills over 111,000 people a year in the United Kingdom.

Deaths from coronary heart disease 139,961
of which 18% were smoking related

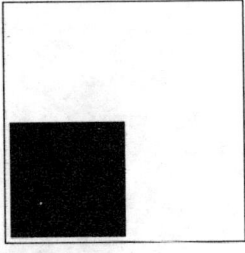

Deaths from lung cancer 32,169
of which 81% were smoking related

Deaths from chronic bronchitis, emphysema
and related diseases 25,511
of which 76% were smoking related

Lung cancer
The more cigarettes per day you smoke and the longer you stay a smoker, the greater your risk of getting lung cancer:

Cigarette consumption and the risk of lung cancer

Number smoked per day	Degree of risk
1 to 14	8 times that a non-smoker
15 to 24	13 times that of a non-smoker
25+	25 times that of a non-smoker

Coronary heart disease

Smoking is the main risk factor for coronary heart disease which you yourself can change. A cigarette smoker runs at least two or three times the risk of having a heart attack than a non-smoker.

And if a smoker has raised blood cholesterol and high blood pressure as well, then the risk of a heart attack can be as much as eight times that of a non-smoker. If your grandfather, father, or other close relations have heart disease, your smoking will greatly increase your inherited risk of heart disease.

Bronchitis and emphysema

Nine out of ten deaths from chronic bronchitis and emphysema (a disease which destroys the walls of the air sacs in the lungs) are caused by smoking.

How giving up smoking reduces your risks

When you give up smoking, your relative risk of getting lung cancer starts dropping, so that after 10 to 15 years your risk is only slightly greater than that of someone who has never smoked.

Similarly, after 10 to 15 years of not smoking, your relative risk of a heart attack is reduced almost to the level of a life-long non-smoker.

The costs

To encourage you to give up, work out how much you would spend in your working lifetime on cigarettes, then think of all the things you could do with that money:

A new year, a new you

The financial cost

Age now

Retirement age

Number of years to retirement

Amount spent on cigarettes each day   £

Amount spent on cigarettes each week   £

Amount spent on cigarettes each year   £

Amount that will be spent on cigarettes up to retirement*   £

* Remember that this is at today's prices.

The health costs

About one in four people who smoke are killed by it before their time. Don't let it be you.

Women who smoke when they are pregnant run a greater risk of miscarriage or of their baby being born premature or underweight.

Smoking increases your risk of heart disease, emphysema and other ilnesses.

Nicotine reaches the brain 7 seconds after inhaling. In small amounts it stimulates nerve impulses in large amounts it inhibits them. Its effect on mood and behaviour are also complex.

Preparing to stop

Understanding your habit

In order to help you give up it is a good idea to keep a diary of when and where you smoke. Fill in the diary opposite.

A smoke-free year?

Smoker's diary

I think I usually smoke……cigarettes a day	**How many**			
When I smoked	**Fri**	**Sat**	**Sun**	**Mon**
First thing – in bed				
Getting up				
At breakfast				
Travelling to work				
Starting work				
When a problem came up				
Answering the phone				
In the loo				
At tea/coffee break				
With a meal (except breakfast)				
After a meal				
Waiting to meet someone				
Over a drink				
While driving				
While reading				
Doing the housework				
At the shops				
At the pub				
Watching TV				
Last thing at night				
After making love				
Other times*				
Total smoked				

*Write in your own 'special' times.

You will see from your completed diary that your smoking is strongly linked to certain times and situations – the first smoke of the day, when the phone rings. Change your habits – break the link between the situation and smoking.

Getting help

Most people manage to stop smoking without any special assistance. But some people need that bit of extra help to get them through it. You might wish to consider:

- Attending a smoking cessation course – ask your GP or local health education unit whether there are any in your area.
- Hypnotherapy if you really can't summon up enough will-power on your own.
- Nicotine replacement therapy – chewing gum or patches.

Stopping

The big day has arrived. You've decided to stop. And you do stop. What about those withdrawal symptoms you've heard people talk about. After all, nicotine is an addictive drug, isn't it? How will you cope?

Well, there are some things you can do to help:

- Drink plenty of liquids (but not tea, coffee or alcohol) to flush the nicotine out of your body.
- Do regular deep breathing. It will help increase your lung capacity – no bad thing after all that smoking.
- Get more physically active. Start gently and build up. There are hints on exercise in another section of this book.
- Try to relax. (See page 78)
- Make sure you change your routine.
- Find something to take your mind off it.

It's worth keeping a diary during the first few weeks so that you can keep a check on your own progress. Make a note of every day that passes without a cigarette. The more days that pass, the easier it becomes. Nothing succeeds like success. You'll grow in confidence.

But be careful. Don't let anyone persuade you to take a cigarette. Just one can set you back to square one. You're a non-smoker now and don't you forget it.

And just look at all that money you're saving. Why not put it in a jar for the first four weeks and see it mount up. Then go out and treat yourself.

Staying stopped

Fantastic. The craving has gone. You're no longer a nicotine addict. You've got more cash in your pocket. You smell better. You feel better.

A new year, a new you

You're a non-smoker now and don't you forget it

Now's the time for a bit of "true grit". You need to resist all the temptations and make sure you stay stopped. Of course, you'll still think about cigarettes. But you've won the psychological battle and are well placed to stay on top of things.

Here's a non-smoker's charter for you to abide by:

- Every time you feel a little twinge, remind yourself how much healthier you are.
- Count up the pounds you've saved since you stopped. Spend the money on something else instead – something that you'll enjoy without it doing you any harm.
- Keep away from smoky atmospheres if you can. You don't want to breathe other people's smoke.

The benefits of giving up

When the daily assault of nicotine, carbon monoxide, tar and other poisons has stopped, the body begins to repair the damage. These benefits follow:

- Hair, skin and breath no longer smell of tobacco smoke.
- The natural decline in efficiency of the lungs slows down to a rate similar to the non-smoker.
- Sense of taste and smell improves.
- Breathing improves.
- More able to cope with sudden exertion.
- Reduction in phlegm and loss of smoker's cough.
- No worry over damage smoking is doing health.
- Feeling good about yourself for having stopped.
- Reduction of risk of smoking related diseases.

Giving up smoking increases the chances of living a longer and healthier life.

Beating stress

You're feeling uptight and stressed out – most of us have at some time experienced at least some of the tell-tale signs of that – anxiety, tension, frustration, not sleeping, bad eating habits, exhaustion, lack of concentration, being more accident prone, and loss of self-esteem. These are the effects of the harmful type of stress. But not all types of stress are harmful. A challenge can be beneficial and stimulating; it can increase energy, drive and productivity enabling us to tackle the problem successfully, and feel exhilarated afterwards by our achievement. We need a challenge and stimulation. Too little work or responsibility can be just as stressful as having too much – the trick is to find the right level.

Beating stress

Are you stressed

Do you   **Yes**   **No**

Feel near to tears much of the time?

Find it hard to concentrate and make decisions?

Shout at people around you at home and at work?

Feel tired most of the time?

Have no interest in sex?

Sleep badly?

Feel stretched beyond your limits at the end of the day?

Drink and smoke more to help you get through?

Feel that you just can't cope?

Eat when you're not hungry?

Feel you have achieved nothing of value at the end of the day?

If you answer 'yes' to more than four of these questions, you are stressed. *Do* something about it.

The first thing you need to do is to recognise what is causing the stress and explore ways of changing it. Any major change in life, some of them pleasant, can create stress. It is when too many of these come together that there are problems. Challenges you can meet easily at one time in your life may make for stress at another.

A new year, a new you

Some causes of stress

- Debt/money problems/mortgage
- Job loss/job change
- Death of somebody we love and/or need
- Ending or beginning of a relationship
- Having a baby/not having a baby
- Moving home/living somewhere you don't like
- Being discriminated against because of race, class, age etc
- Any illness especially one for which you can find no appropriate treatment
- Poor diet – low in fresh foods and high in sugar, white flour, caffeine additives and salt
- Poor living/working conditions
- Getting married/not getting married
- Loneliness
- Caring for an elderly relative or dependent/ having no one to care for
- Too much work/too little work
- Conflict with colleagues/neighbours
- Problems with friends or family
- Fear of redundancy/actual redundancy
- Trouble with your boss
- Children leaving home/children still living at home
- Divorce
- Partner or you stopping work
- Retirement

Do any of these apply to you? If you can say yes to several of these, then watch out. It could be your health is at risk.

Learn to recognise when your muscles are tensed

The body language of stress

When a person is under sudden stress, the body can react in the following ways:

   Heart beats faster

   Muscles tense

   Blood pressure rises

   Breathing becomes faster and shallower

   The liver releases sugar, cholesterol, and fatty acids into the blood

A new year, a new you

Adrenaline flow increases

Sweating increases

Likely to get infections

Digestion slows down

Feelings of anger or anxiety rise

Needless to say, too much of that, too often can seriously damage your health.

Health problems which may result from stress

- Migraine/headache
- Muscular tension
    Backache
    Stiff neck and shoulders
    Aches and pains
- Cardiovascular disorders
    High blood pressure
    Heart attack
    Stroke
- Respiratory disorders
    Asthma
- Digestive disorders
    Peptic ulcers
    Irritable bowel syndrome
    Constipation
    Diarrhoea
- Mental disorders
    Depression
    Anxiety
    Nervous Breakdown
- Accidents
- Poor sleeping habits
- Susceptibility to colds, influenza or other illnesses.
- Menstrual disorders in women

Simple ways of coping with stress

You cannot wave a magic wand and make all your problems go away. But you can take time to sit back and take stock – sort out the real problems from the not so real – to get things in perspective.

Take a blank piece of paper and try to write down:

- Exactly what is making you feel stressed. Why and how you can change it.
- Make a list of things you have to do in order of urgency and do things in that order. Be realistic – are there, perhaps, things you can strike off that list altogether?

Are there, perhaps, things you can strike off your list altogether?

A new year, a new you

- Take regular exercise – gentle, rhythmic exercise like swimming, walking or jogging are all great stress-busters. (Don't use the old excuse that you haven't got time – you'll think and work more efficiently in a less stressed state!)
- Don't try and cope with stress by drinking, smoking or compulsive eating – they might seem to help at the time, but in the long run they lead to yet more stress – and poor health into the bargain.
- Set a limit on the number of hours you work .
- Use stress positively and channel your energy into making your life better.
- Eat regular and healthy meals.
- Learn to relax. Easier said than done, you might say – but there are a number of simple relaxation techniques which you can use to help you unwind. Look for 'Look After Yourself' classes in your area which will show you how to make relaxation a part of your life.

Relaxation exercises

The following exercises will get you started

Deep breathing

Learn to recognise when your muscles are tensed; feel the tension with your fingertips.

1 Sit with your feet flat on the floor, or lie in a comfortable and supported position. Rest your hands lightly on your thighs.
2 Put one hand on your chest and the other on your stomach and breathe slowly and deeply through your nose. If you are breathing correctly, your stomach, not your chest, should rise at the start of each breath.
3 As you breathe, gradually drop your shoulders and relax your hands. Make sure your teeth are not tightly clenched.

It takes a bit of practice but when you have mastered the art of calm, controlled breathing and are able to release unnecessary muscular tension at will during the day, you will have developed a very useful technique for combating stressful moments in your life.

An exercise for relaxing the mind.

When your body is relaxed and heavy, it is useful to focus your mind on something pleasant so that it is prevented from thinking about everyday things which worry us.

Try thinking of one of these, perhaps just for one minute to start with, building up to about five minutes over a period of time. Imagine every little detail – the sights, sounds, scents, colours, etc.

A vase of flowers.
A picture or a painting.
A room in your house.
Imagine you are going for a walk.
Look around a garden you know well.
A field of corn or trees blowing in the wind.
A harbour with little boats bobbing in the breeze.
Use your ears and listen to the sounds around you.
Say 'one' mentally every time you breathe out.

If everyday thoughts come into your mind to disturb you, just note them mentally and let them pass. Don't hang on to them but bring your attention back to your chosen topic.

Deep Relaxation Exercise

1. Sit quietly in a comfortable position, feet flat on the floor. Arms uncrossed.
2. Close your eyes breathe slowly and deeply. Concentrate on the breathing movements in your chest, back and stomach.

Feet and legs

3. Concentrate first on your feet. Curl the toes downwards, as if digging them into sand. Feel the tension in your toes.
4. Now relax your toes. Notice the difference from the feeling of tension that you felt a few seconds ago.
5. Now the calf muscles: point your toes back towards your chest. Feel the tension in the lower part of your leg. Hold it like that.
6. Now relax.

A new year, a new you

7 Concentrate on the muscles in your thighs. Lift your legs up from the chair, holding them straight out in the air. Visualise your muscle fibres stretched and tense.

8 Suddenly let your feet and legs relax. Your feet feel soft and floppy and your legs feel heavy and lazy. Keep breathing slowly and deeply.

Back

9 Pull your shoulders back and arch your back away from the chair. Hold it like that.

10 Now relax back into the chair.

Stomach

11 Pull your stomach muscles in as far as they will go. Tighten the muscles as though you are preparing to be punched in the stomach.

12 Now relax. Imagine the muscles falling back into place around one another. Notice how comfortable it feels. Breathe slowly and deeply.

Hands

13 Next concentrate on the hands. Clench your fists as hard as you can. Notice the feelings of tension in your fingers, your thumb, the palm of your hand, your knuckles and the back of your hand. Notice how clenching your fist makes your arms tense as well.

14 Now, let your hands relax. Let them feel loose and floppy.

Arms

15 Rest your arms on your knees with the back of your hands facing up.

16 Bend you hand at the wrist. Point your fingers straight up in the air. Feel the tension in the backs of your hands and forearms.

17 Now relax. Keep breathing slowly and deeply.

18 Flex the muscles in your upper right arm by trying to touch your right shoulder with your right wrist. Tighten your biceps.

19 Now relax.

20 Repeat it with the left arm.

Shoulders

21 Tense the muscles by hunching your shoulders.
22 Bring your shoulders up as if to touch your ears. Notice how your breathing is affected.
23 Now relax. Let your arms become soft and heavy again and let your shoulders slump as low as possible. Your breathing becomes slow and regular again.

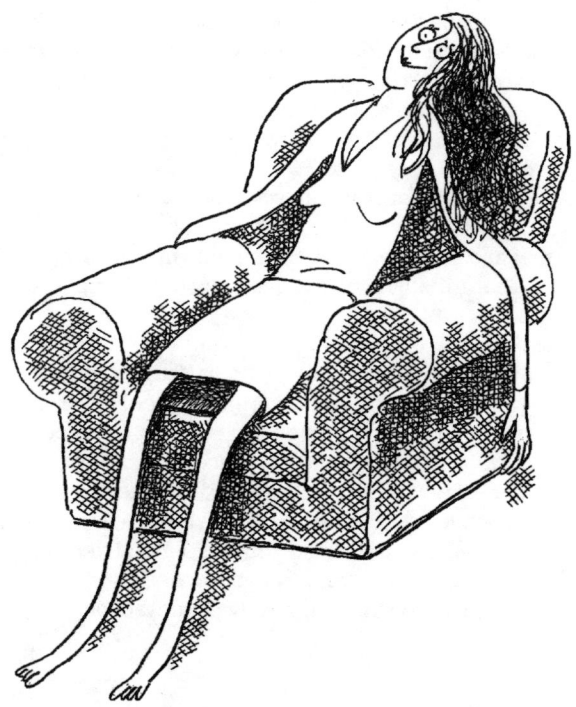

Taking you deeper and deeper into relaxation

Neck

24 Tense your neck muscles by pushing your head back. Notice the feelings of tension in the back of your neck, back of your head and across your shoulders. Notice the tension in the front of your neck and around your jaw and the lower part of your face.

25 Now bring your head forward and suddenly let your neck muscles relax. Your head drops forward and feels floppy and heavy. Your breathing becomes slower and regular.

Face

26 Begin by frowning and creasing your forehead.

27 Now add to the tension by closing your eyes as tightly as you can. Notice the feelings of tension you are producing.

28 Make your face still more tense by clenching your jaws, pursing your lips and pressing your tongue against the roof of your mouth. Feel the tension in your cheeks and around your face.

29 Suddenly relax your face muscles. Notice the skin becoming soft as your forehead and cheeks return to normal and your jaw sags. Your mouth may be slightly open. Your breathing once again returns to normal.

The whole body

30 Now there is no tension in your body. You are relaxed. Concentrate on all the muscle areas and feel how relaxed they are. Let go of any tension that remains. Your toes.. calves.. thighs.. back.. stomach.. hands.. arms.. shoulders.. neck.. face. Let yourself feel relaxed. Breathe slowly. As each breath leaves your body, it's carrying away more and more tension and taking you deeper and deeper into relaxation. Finish gradually. Let your muscles get ready to move again as you think 'Three, two, one, action.'

Reducing your key health risks

No-one can go through life risk-free. Many things that happen to us are unpredictable and many couldn't have been avoided. But on the positive side, there's a lot we can do to reduce risks to our health. The other sections of this book take a close look at the impact of smoking, alcohol, food, physical activity and stress on our lives and show what we can do to take control. Here, we look at some of the other risks we run and what, through common sense, we can do to reduce them as far as possible.

Be aware of your body

That's the starting point for reducing your risks – of cancer, of heart disease and of infections that can be passed on through sex.

It's amazing how little many people really know about their own bodies and how infrequently they take a good look at themselves.

Nobody's suggesting, though, that you should spend hours each day examining every nook and cranny to look for tell-tale signs of cancer. But being generally aware of your body – and how its functioning – is one way of helping to reduce your risks, because you're more likely to spot things before they go too far.

And if you think you've spotted something amiss, then make an early appointment to go and see your doctor. Don't put it off. The sooner, the better. Early detection means that treatment can be successfull.

A new year, a new you

Reducing your risk of cancer

Many cancers can be treated successfully and there are steps which we can all take to either reduce our risk of developing the disease, or of discovering it early when it may be easier to treat.

Checklist of ways to protect yourself

1 Don't smoke. 81% of lung cancers are the result of smoking.
2 Protect yourself in the sun. Use the right sunscreen for your skin. Tan gradually, don't burn. Avoid the midday sun or

'I told you to use a higher SPF, Kevin'

Reducing your key health risks

cover up with loose clothing and a hat. Experts believe that the increase in both types of skin cancer could be reduced by us taking more care in the sun.

3 Eat wisely. A diet rich in starch and fibre and low in fat with plenty of fruit and vegetables will help to protect you. It is thought that 35% of all cancers are caused by dietary factors.

4 Take precautions if you work with dangerous chemicals or other materials. Follow the instructions for use and wear protective clothing.

5 Be aware of any changes in your body and if you suspect that something is not right get it checked by your doctor. The earlier cancers are treated the less likely they are to spread.

Be aware checklist

Look out for:

1 A lump anywhere in your body which you can't explain (particularly, for women, in the breast; and for men, in the testicles).

2 A change in a skin mole – bleeding or extreme itchiness, for example

3 A sore that doesn't show signs of healing up and just seems to stay there.

4 A persistent cough or hoarseness in the throat – something you just can't seem to shake off that easily.

5 Persistent indigestion or difficulty in swallowing.

6 Vomiting or coughing up blood.

7 Changes in your normal bowel habits (e.g., persistent diarrhoea or constipation).

8 Any bleeding in the urine or bowel movement. For women any abnormal vaginal bleeding – either between your periods or after you have had the menopause.

9 Unexplained weight loss.

10 Unexplained loss of appetite.

There could be many reasons for these symptoms. It doesn't necessarily mean there's something wrong or that it's an early sign of cancer. But you should certainly keep an eye on the situation and go and see your doctor if it looks as though the problem is not going away of its own accord.

Reducing the risk of heart disease

1. Increase the level of your fitness by becoming more active.
2. Give up smoking. 20 cigarettes a day doubles your risk of heart disease.
3. Eat well and drink alcohol sensibly. Reduce the fat and sugar in your diet and increase the amounts of fruit, vegetables, starch and fibre. This will help to control your weight, reduce the level of cholesterol and reduce blood pressure.
4. If you are under stress try to change the situation and do some relaxation exercises.
5. If you know there is a family history of heart disease make sure you do everything possible to reduce your risk, and get regular check ups.

Reducing your risk of catching sexually transmitted diseases

Sex can be good for your health. It's a natural way of sharing affection and tenderness, as well as putting a bit of sparkle and excitement into your life.

Sex can boost your morale, reduce your stress level – and keep you feeling young. Sex has got a lot going for it. Whatever your relationship, sex should be healthy, fun – and, above all, safe.

Why do we need safer sex

Added to the age old worry of unplanned pregnancy is the risk of sexually transmitted infections (including, for example, herpes, hepatitis, gonorrhea and HIV – the virus that causes AIDS). Having safer sex takes the worry out of sex because you know that you are helping to prevent pregnancy and protect yourself and your partner against infections.

What is safer sex?

Having sex without using a condom increases the chance of infection and pregnancy. Safer sex simply involves giving and getting sexual pleasure in ways which don't put us or our partners at risk of unplanned pregnancy or STDs (sexually transmitted diseases), including HIV. This can include exploring alternatives to penetration, using condoms and broadening the range of our sexual activity.

Condoms, male or female, can also protect against cancer of the cervix (neck of the womb) it makes sense to use them.

Properly tested condoms have passed the strict tests of the British Standards Institution (BSI), so choose one with the Kitemark on the pack.

A new year, a new you

Safer sex checklist

Don't have sex without a condom to please your partner.

Respect yourself – and value your health – even if your partner doesn't.

Do take the initiative.

Carry your own condoms. Don't rely on the other person. Better for both of you to be prepared than neither.

Do put sexual health first.

Your first priority is protecting one another's health. This needn't interfere with sexual enjoyment.

Explore other ways to share sexual pleasure.

We tend to think that lovemaking has to end with a man's penis inside his partner. But there are plenty of other ways to share sexual pleasure apart from penetration.

Be sensible.

Don't have sex if you or your partner has a sore or discharge. Get help if you notice anything unusual.

Practice makes perfect.

If you haven't used a condom before, try handling one or practising on your own.

Health at work

Back trouble is a major cause of disability in people under forty-five and second only to colds in terms of time lost from work. There a number of things which you can do to help to prevent back injury.

1. Improve your level of physical fitness. This will increase your flexibility and the strengthen your muscles.
2. Make sure that you always bend your knees and lift things close to the body not at full stretch.
3. Lift small amounts rather than large. For example don't lift a full spade when digging the garden.
4. Ensure that your bed is not too soft. It should support the body and not sag.
5. Improve your work station. Are the chair/desk the the right height? The back of the chair should support you and your feet should be on the floor and the desk/ keyboard at elbow level. Place things where you don't have to twist to reach them.
6. Work to improve your posture.

Repetitive strain injury

This is the result of repetitive muscular contraction, usually in the hand or forearm. It is often associated with work on a computer screen. You should plan you work so that you take regular breaks and don't carry on the same task for long periods.

Change your position regularly and don't spend more than 75% of the day on the keyboard.

A new year, a new you

Take control – it's your body

As well as being aware of your body, you need to take control - of your lifestyle and how, through that lifestyle, you're treating your body.

Taking control is, of course, very much an attitude of mind. It's you telling yourself that you want to do certain things – and then doing them. Yes, we all have lapses. We're human. But many of the risks we run in life are self-imposed and can be avoided.

The ten-point taking control formula

You want to be in control of your lifestyle. How well do you score on these ten points?

1. You've given up smoking and don't intend to start again. Better still, you've never smoked anyway.
2. You're now quite physically active on a regular basis – which means vigorous, energetic activity at least three times a week for up to 20 minutes at a time, or building up to 30 minutes of activity during the day. You will be improving your strength and suppleness at the same time.
3. You're eating a diet that's rich in fibre and low in fatty foods and sugar. And you're happy with that diet and think you're capable of sticking to it more or less permanently. In other words, it's not just a passing fad while you try and lose a few pounds.
4. If you drink alcohol, you're managing to keep within a weekly limit of 21 units (for men) or 14 units (for women). You keep a mental note of what you're drinking these days and conscientiously stick to the rules.
5. You recognise when you're under stress and take active steps to deal with the stress before it affects you. You've learned to relax – and you find time to relax, despite your hectic schedule.

6 In your sexual relationships, you take precautions against infections that can be passed on. Using a condom is the best way for people who don't know one another's histories very

well to avoid the risk of HIV and AIDS and other diseases such as hepatitis. If that applies to you, do you always use a condom now? And bear in mind the fact that the fewer partners you have, the less your risk of a sexually transmitted infection. You enjoy your sex life but you're in control.

7 You're aware of the dangers of too much sunshine for the skin – its a major cause of skin cancer. So you don't stay out in it for hours without proper protection. Haven't you seen how the Aussie cricketers take the sun very seriously these days? You may be a sun worshipper but you're not silly.

8 You consult your doctor if you think there's a problem brewing on any of the risk factors listed earlier in this chapter. Doctors don't mind checking up. They believe in prevention where it's possible through early detection of symptoms. But don't take it to extremes. Doctors don't want to see you every week.

9 You respond positively to any invitations from your doctor to attend the surgery for a check up or screening (breast or cervical cancer for women; a "Well Person" clinic for either of the sexes).

10 Finally, you now look on health as something you can influence.

Progress chart

How have you been doing? Here's a chart on which you can record your achievements over the year. Keeping a record is a good way of staying committed to the healthier you.

Weight	Units of alcohol per week	Cigarettes smoked	Minutes of physical activity
JANUARY			
Week 1			
Week 2			
Week 3			
Week 4			
FEBRUARY			
Week 1			
Week 2			
Week 3			
Week 4			

Progress chart

Weight	Units of alcohol per week	Cigarettes smoked	Minutes of physical activity
MARCH			
Week 1			
Week 2			
Week 3			
Week 4			
APRIL			
Week 1			
Week 2			
Week 3			
Week 4			
MAY			
Week 1			
Week 2			
Week 3			
Week 4			

A new year, a new you

Weight	Units of alcohol per week	Cigarettes smoked	Minutes of physical activity
JUNE			
Week 1			
Week 2			
Week 3			
Week 4			
JULY			
Week 1			
Week 2			
Week 3			
Week 4			
AUGUST			
Week 1			
Week 2			
Week 3			
Week 4			

Progress chart

Weight	Units of alcohol per week	Cigarettes smoked	Minutes of physical activity

SEPTEMBER

Week 1

Week 2

Week 3

Week 4

OCTOBER

Week 1

Week 2

Week 3

Week 4

NOVEMBER

Week 1

Week 2

Week 3

Week 4

A new year, a new you

Weight	Units of alcohol per week	Cigarettes smoked	Minutes of physical activity
DECEMBER			
Week 1			
Week 2			
Week 3			
Week 4			

Major achievements

My six biggest achievements over the year in changing my lifestyle for the better have been:

1
2
3
4
5
6

Well done. But now is not the time to relax. You need to make sure the 'New You' becomes the permanent you.